DATE DUE

GAYLORD		PRINTED IN U.S.A.

A Call for Change in Teacher Education

U. S.
**NATIONAL
COMMISSION
FOR EXCELLENCE
IN TEACHER
EDUCATION**

The issuance of this report is a milestone in the continuing dialogue on teacher education. Many, including some Commissioners, have concerns and recommendations that go beyond those contained here. The report provides a context for bringing about change and improvements in teacher education.

Support for the National Commission for Excellence in Teacher Education and the publication of this document was provided by:

The U.S. Department of Education

The National Institute of Education

The Ford Foundation

The Hewlett Foundation

The Lilly Endowment, Inc.

The University of Texas at Austin,
College of Education

The opinions, conclusions, and recommendations expressed in this report are those of the National Commission for Excellence in Teacher Education; they are not necessarily those of the funding sources or of the American Association of Colleges for Teacher Education. AACTE is printing and distributing this document to stimulate discussion, study, and improvement of teacher education.

Copies of
A Call for Change in Teacher Education
may be ordered from
The American Association of Colleges for Teacher Education
One Dupont Circle, Suite 610
Washington, DC 20036

Single copy (prepaid) $7.00

First printing: February 1985
Second Printing: October 1987

Library of Congress Catalog Card No.: 85–60490

International Standard Book Number: 0-89333-035-3

Contents

220069

Members of the National Commission for Excellence in Teacher Education

Dr. C. Peter Magrath,
Commission Chair
President, University of Missouri
Columbia, Missouri

Dr. J. Myron Atkin
Dean, School of Education
Stanford University
Stanford, California

Dr. Frank B. Brouillet
State Superintendent
  of Public Instruction
Olympia, Washington

Dr. John E. Brown
President, Coe College
Cedar Rapids, Iowa

The Honorable Stephen Cobb
Representative, Tennessee
  General Assembly
Nashville, Tennessee

Ms. Mary Hatwood Futrell
President, National Education
  Association
Washington, D.C.

The Honorable
  Robert D. Graham
Governor of Florida
Tallahassee, Florida

Dr. Mari-Luci Jaramillo
Associate Dean,
  College of Education
The University of New Mexico
Albuquerque, New Mexico

Dr. Jonathan C. Messerli
President, Muhlenberg College
Allentown, Pennsylvania

The Honorable
 Howard C. Nielson
Representative in Congress
Provo, Utah

Dr. M. Joan Parent
Immediate Past President,
 National School Boards
 Association
Foley, Minnesota

Dr. W. Ann Reynolds
Chancellor, The California State
 University System
Long Beach, California

Dr. J. T. Sandefur
Dean, College of Education
Western Kentucky University
Bowling Green, Kentucky

Sister Michelle Schiffgens, Ph.D.
Chair, Division of
 Education/
 Physical Education/
 Psychology
Marycrest College
Davenport, Iowa

Mr. Albert Shanker
President, American Federation
 of Teachers
Washington, D.C.

Dr. Mark Shibles
Dean, School of Education
University of Connecticut
Storrs, Connecticut

Dr. Richard C. Wallace, Jr.
Superintendent of Schools
Pittsburgh, Pennsylvania

A Letter to the Nation: A Call for Change

The much-acclaimed *A Nation at Risk,* released to the American public in April 1983, called upon "all segments of our population" and especially "groups with an interest in and responsibility for education reform" to respond with recommendations. This report of the National Commission for Excellence in Teacher Education provides, we believe, a significant reply.

Our response is a call for change in meeting the vital challenge to improve the preparation of teachers and to make teaching a more rewarding and desirable profession. The urgency for such reform has been recognized increasingly in recent years, but only minimal attention has been given to the challenges of recruiting, preparing, and retaining qualified teachers.

This report highlights five related issues: (1) supply and demand for quality teachers, (2) content of teacher education programs, (3) accountability for teacher education, (4) resource requirements for teacher education programs, and (5) conditions necessary to support the highest quality of teaching. A broad analysis of each of the issues is provided, supported by selected empirical findings. Finally, a series of sixteen recommendations is proposed to address the need for change and improvement.

The authors of the report are members of the National Commission for Excellence in Teacher Education. Their professional backgrounds and responsibilities vary considerably; so, too, do their views on teaching and teacher education. The Commissioners do not necessarily agree on every detail describing the problems or the proposed solutions. Be assured, though, that each one stands behind the recommendations in this report and is thoroughly committed to major improvements in teacher education.

The Commission was proposed and initiated by the American Association of Colleges for Teacher Education, the leading professional organization for schools that prepare and train teachers. The study was partially funded through a discretionary grant from U.S. Secretary of Education T.H. Bell. From May 1984 through January 1985, the Commissioners met three times, conducted five two-day hearings across the country, solicited 30 research papers from educational experts, and reviewed the testimony of more than 70 witnesses. These items are listed in the appendices

This report, which emerged from these many sources, is more than an assessment of a troubled profession and educational system. It is also a call for change, a call that can only be answered by public policy makers, academic communities, local schools, teacher organizations, and— ultimately and most importantly—by the American public.

Change has its price; failure to change is even more expensive. I urge our fellow citizens to respond to our call for reform in a forceful, timely fashion. At stake is not the present status of teachers but the future of the nation. To paraphrase Henry Brooks Adams, Teachers affect eternity; they can never tell where their influence stops.

C. PETER MAGRATH
CHAIR, NATIONAL COMMISSION
FOR EXCELLENCE IN TEACHER EDUCATION

February 1985

A Call for Change in Teacher Education

The National Commission for Excellence in Teacher Education was guided by two charges: to become well informed about the teacher education enterprise along with efforts to improve teacher education programs, and to recommend to policymakers and college and university leaders ways to improve the enterprise.

Several assumptions emerged from the meetings, hearings, and seminars that the Commission held:

First, the Commission report could fill a void left by other commissions and study groups that have published reports about American education during the past twenty months. Although most of the reports referred to teacher education and the quality of teachers, few focused on how prospective teachers are recruited, educated, employed, and assigned, or on how new teachers develop into fully competent professionals. We believe this report fills those gaps.

Second, every part of a teacher's education—from the liberal arts programs of the prospective teacher to the continuing education of the veteran—can be improved; even the best existing programs are not good enough. Yet, we recognize that many efforts to improve are underway, and we urge that these be supported and reinforced.

Third, teaching is a complex human endeavor guided by knowledge that is both scientific and artistic. Teachers are professionals, not merely technicians. They do not simply follow directions in a teacher's manual or obey instructions from principals or supervisors. Using a knowledge base acquired through study, research, and practice, teachers continually make complex decisions about the curriculum, the students, and instruction. Their knowledge of the subject to be taught must go beyond mastery of facts; teachers must understand what information is appropriate to teach to youngsters of different ages and how that information is best taught and learned. Professional teachers also understand the numerous educational issues that confront today's schools, and they can explain these to parents and other interested citizens. We believe that teachers must be such professionals.

Fourth, schools will remain prominent institutions in American society, and their traditional roles and responsibilities will persist. Children and young people will continue to spend a major portion of their lives in schools, studying individually and in groups. Although new technologies and alternative resources for schooling will complement and enrich—not detract from—a school's curriculum and the teacher's role in it, learning at home through a computer will not replace schools. Similarly, other teaching resources in a community—museums, galleries, concert halls, libraries, social and service agencies, and businesses—should supplement, but not supplant, teachers.

Fifth, the education of prospective teachers will continue to be centered in colleges and universities, which provide structure for the systematic study of organized bodies of knowledge as well as the scholarly inquiry and intellectual discourse that are integral to the education of all professions. We believe it essential that higher education institutions strengthen their commitments to the preparation of excellent teachers. We also believe that the connections between colleges and schools should be significantly improved, because it is in the schools where practicing teachers serve the primary instructing, modeling, planning, and monitoring roles in teacher education.

teacher education is not a single, time-bound activity, but a continuing process of career development

Sixth, teacher education is not a single, time-bound activity, but a continuing process of career development. Teachers have a right to expect superior initial preparation that provides them with the knowledge and skills to enter the field; they also have a right to expect systematic evaluation, feedback, and support during the first years of teaching and an integrated program for continued professional development. The provision of career development opportunities for teachers is the shared responsibility of the entire education community—school districts, higher education, professional organizations, and the states.

Seventh, education is primarily a state, not a federal, function. The responsibility for teacher education will remain with the states, which will continue to be accountable to their citizens for the quality and the success of teacher education programs. Although the federal government has a compelling interest in the well-being of the nation's schools (and it has both defined educational issues of national interest and funded programs that serve those interests), it has neither advocated nor prescribed curricula, and it has set no standards for teaching or for schools. It should not do so.

Education and democracy in America have been intertwined since our nation's birth. Thomas Jefferson affirmed the need for an educated citizenry in 1779, when he proposed a system of common schools in Virginia. Education, as Jefferson believed, is necessary to illuminate the minds of the people and to give them the best protection against the dangers of authoritarian government. A hundred and thirty-five years later, John Dewey's classic *Democracy and Education* reaffirmed the interdependence of school and society. We still believe that education enables people both to fulfil their personal aspirations and to contribute to the vitality of the democratic society of which they are a part.

Teacher education takes its direction from Jefferson's vision of a people who are free because they are schooled in the responsibilities and benefits of a democratic society. From the origin of the normal school in New England and the first university programs for teacher education more than a century ago, this interdependence of school and society has shaped the focus and content of training programs. Teacher educators have prepared succeeding generations of teachers to promote both the well-being of the individual and the betterment of society.

Schools, which bring together children; teachers and other school personnel, who make professional services available; and teacher education, which prepares the people to serve the profession and the schools, form a mutually beneficial alliance for society's gain. The schools, the teaching profession, and teacher education all must fill their respective responsibilities in a manner to enhance the others and society.

Themes and Recommendations

This report offers a vision of a professional teacher who can lead to the transformation of the schools and enrich the lives of young people. To produce such teachers, changes in the content, time, delivery, and rigor of teacher education are needed; new patterns of candidate recruitment and professional development are needed; and vastly changed and improved conditions for teaching in the schools are needed.

The report is organized around the following themes: (1) supply and demand for quality teachers, (2) programs for teacher education, (3) accountability for teacher education, (4) resources for teacher education, and (5) conditions necessary to support the highest quality of teaching. Each theme is discussed, along with selected findings, and our recommendations are presented at the close of each section.

We offer you our best judgments about the problems confronting American teacher education. Our recommendations require action by policymakers and academic leaders. We believe their actions will be in the best interests of the next generation of students—and they are vital to our nation's strength.

Supply and Demand for Quality Teachers

Teacher education has been criticized perhaps most consistently and severely because of the quality of those admitted to and graduated from its programs. The most frequently cited index of quality is the college admission test scores of high school seniors who say they plan to become teachers; their scores are lower and have dropped farther than the scores of their peers planning to pursue other fields of study. We found such evidence, but we also found conflicting evidence, as the following statistics show:

High school seniors who said they planned to enter teaching scored in the bottom quartile of all those taking the American College Testing (ACT) program examination, and ranked fifteenth out of nineteen fields.

The high school grade point average of prospective teachers was virtually the same—3.03 versus 3.09—as for those not interested in teaching careers.

No significant differences in grade point averages for the first two years of college was found for prospective teachers versus those not planning to teach. During this part of the college program, all students take essentially the same courses.

A 1982-83 study of graduates from Washington state colleges and universities found that 61% of those earning teaching certificates had grade averages at or above the average grade for all graduates. Only 11% had grades in the bottom one-fifth of all graduates.

Now that governors, state legislatures, and commissions have begun corrective steps, two external forces threaten to make the recruitment of able teacher candidates more difficult than ever before. The first is demographic:

5

By 1990, the number of 18-year-olds will be 0.8 million fewer than in 1980; thus the pool from which teacher education can recruit students will be reduced. At the same time, the number of preschool and elementary school children will increase. The second force is social: The opening of new career opportunities to minorities and women has encouraged many talented people, who formerly would have become teachers, to enter other professions. We found the following evidence:

The annual number of births in the United States advanced from a mid-Depression low of fewer than 2.4 million to a post-Korean War high of more than 4.2 million. This number decreased to approximately 3.1 million by the mid-1970s, but has since grown to more than 3.6 million.

By 1990 the United States will need a million new teachers. If traditional teacher education programs are the only source of teachers, then one in ten college students will have to enroll in teacher education programs to meet national requirements. In 1982 fewer than one in twenty entering freshmen listed teaching as a probable career occupation—a decrease from almost one in five in 1970.

Minorities constitute 26% of the American school population; yet, they comprise less than 12.5% of the K-12 teaching force. By the 1990s, the respective figures are projected to be 30% and 5%.

Because of demographic and social forces, American education is moving rapidly from a surplus to a shortage of teachers. The shortage will not be uniform; it will be more acute in some sections of the country, more pronounced in some disciplines, and more serious for some constituencies. No one should misunderstand: This lack of highly qualified, properly trained teachers will be real, and its consequences for the nation ominous. First, in terms of quality, even the diminished numbers of students entering teacher education appear to be drawn disproportionately from the lower half of the entering college class. Second, in terms of impact, the shortages are increasing or developing in fields that other Commissions have identified as crucial—that is, mathematics, science, computers, and foreign languages. The following evidence reveals the impending shortage:

Currently 2.37 million elementary and secondary teachers work in the nation's schools. The number of new teachers entering the profession each year declined from 300,000 in 1972 to fewer than 150,000 in 1982.

In 1981, only 78% of all new teachers were certified or eligible for certification in the fields to which they were assigned. Less than half of all new mathematics and science teachers were certified in those fields.

The 1984 annual survey of teacher placement officers showed that five teaching fields (mathematics, physics, chemistry, computer programming, and data processing) had considerable teacher shortages.

The same 1984 survey when compared with 1983 data for all regions of the continental U.S. showed lower supply in relation to demand. The shortage increased for elementary teachers and for science, Spanish, and French teachers.

To help overcome the shortage of traditional college-age students entering teaching, and to assist in educational reform, a number of reports have suggested that people who want to make midcareer changes into teaching should be helped to do so. Such late entrants include those completing military service or those wanting to transfer skills learned in another profession. Programs should be designed to help these people move into teaching, but the same criteria of competence and performance as in regular programs should apply.

Another source of potential teachers to reduce the coming shortage is that group of teachers who could not find jobs or who taught for a few years and then left the profession. In the states of New York and Washington, estimates are that three out of four newly hired teachers will come from this reserve pool. How large the pool is and how it varies from state to state are unknowns, but the Commission did learn that in Washington, returning teachers typically completed their training a number of years ago. Meanwhile, many states and colleges have developed more rigorous standards and have improved their programs. These returning teachers should have opportunities to update their skills through programs planned cooperatively by the profession, the schools, and higher education institutions.

people who want to make midcareer changes into teaching should be helped to do so . . . but the same criteria of competence and performance as in regular programs should apply

Recommendations
Supply and Demand for Quality Teachers

RECOMMENDATION 1: ADMISSION TO AND GRADUATION FROM TEACHER EDUCATION PROGRAMS SHOULD BE BASED UPON RIGOROUS ACADEMIC AND PERFORMANCE STANDARDS.

In the campaign to attract more students into the teaching profession, quality must not be sacrificed. All teacher candidates should be held to rigorous standards and undergo at least three thorough reviews during the selection and training process. First, before admission into the teacher education program, every candidate should demonstrate above-average collegiate-level scholarship, good critical-thinking skills, and competence in communication skills, particularly reading, writing, and speaking. A variety of methods—paper and pencil tests, interviews, work samples, and the like—should be used to make these determinations. Second, before approval for student teaching, every candidate should demonstrate mastery of both the subject to be taught and the pedagogical foundations that underlie effective teaching. Third, before graduation from a teacher education program, every candidate should demonstrate his or her knowledge and skills on three measures: (a) a test of knowledge of the subject to be taught, (b) a test of knowledge and application of the foundations, science, and processes of teaching, and (c) ability to teach effectively.

RECOMMENDATION 2: THE STATES, IN CONCERT WITH THE FEDERAL GOVERNMENT, SHOULD LAUNCH A NATIONWIDE CAMPAIGN TO RECRUIT QUALIFIED CANDIDATES INTO THE TEACHING PROFESSION.

The gains in improving the quality of teachers are in danger of being lost if school systems give in to the intense pressure to get "warm bodies" into the classrooms. Governors, federal and state legislators, the U.S. Department of Education, school boards, and the public must realize that school systems are not something to be fixed and then forgotten. Schools are not immune to the laws of supply and demand.

Policymakers must commit themselves to retaining and improving the quality of teachers even in the coming shortage. They must be willing to bid for the talents of young people, many of whom now have opportunities that were denied them in the past. Standards must not be lowered, so incentives will have to be raised. The public must be assured that the additional funds are purchasing quality education for children.

Even in times of shortage, school boards and administrators should assign teachers only to areas for which they have been specifically prepared and licensed. To expect equally competent performance in another subject or school level is unrealistic, and it is unfair to teachers and students alike.

A national recruitment effort should be targeted toward the most able candidates whether they are high school students, liberal arts majors, or professionals seeking midcareer changes. Federal and state governments should support recruitment by funding incentives and financial assistance, including scholarships, graduate fellowships, and forgivable loans to academically talented students.

One of the most difficult tasks for teacher education is attracting and retaining capable liberal arts students. Arts and sciences faculty, who generally have a low opinion of teacher education, often actively discourage their best students from teaching careers. We challenge each college and university president to develop and maintain an academic and cultural climate wherein students enrolled in preservice and inservice teacher education are accorded dignity and status comparable to that of students enrolled in other professional programs.

RECOMMENDATION 3: SPECIAL PROGRAMS SHOULD BE DEVELOPED TO ATTRACT CAPABLE MINORITY TEACHER CANDIDATES.

As alternative job opportunities expand and mandatory competency testing increases, the nation is likely to see a further decline in the number of minority teachers in the schools. The results will be a lack of role models for minority students and a severe limitation on cross-cultural exposure for majority children. To reverse the projected decline in numbers of minority teachers, special action is required. Federal and state governments, and private philanthropies should ensure that lack of finances will not bar qualified minority students from entering teacher education programs; parents, teachers, counselors, and principals should encourage minority students to consider careers in teaching; colleges and universities should provide a supportive environment; and, above all, intellectually demanding teacher education programs should prepare graduates to meet certification requirements.

Programs
for Teacher Education

The quality of teacher education programs has been widely criticized, as has their poor performance in setting and enforcing standards. For instance, in a recent poll of teachers, just over half rated their training programs *A* or *B* while the others rated their programs *C* or below. The criticism is valid, and we recognize that excellent teachers for the future require better educational opportunities than many current teachers have received. We also recognize that serious efforts are being made by states, individual colleges and universities, and professional organizations to redesign and improve the programs that prepare teachers. We encourage the continuation of these efforts, but we affirm that they are only a beginning; much more needs to be done. External support and pressure are required if necessary changes are to be made.

We strongly affirm that those entering the teaching profession should have an academic concentration and a genuine liberal education. In effect, those requirements are equivalent to a bachelor's degree.

The further training of a teacher depends on whom the nation wants to see in its classrooms. Do we want teachers whose knowledge of the subject and understanding of human development help them decide which questions among the many they hear have the most intellectual mileage and should occupy class discussion, and which questions are idiosyncratic and best handled without using much class time? Do we want teachers whose knowledge of the subject is so extensive that they recognize the basis for common errors, such as those that students make when trying to learn the binomial theorem? Do we want teachers who can construct and interpret tests that are useful in diagnosing and assessing students' problems? The answers must be yes.

10

Do we want prospective teachers who not only have studied how to organize groups of children, but also have practiced doing so under the tutelage of an effective supervisor, thereby assuring employers that their potential teacher has had some successful experience? We say yes.

Do we want teachers who understand that people through the centuries have had different views of childhood—that Calvin, for instance, had one view of children and Rousseau another? Do we want teachers who understand the origins of our public school system and its role in the nation's development? The answers again are yes.

The only reasonable answer to all of these questions is yes Teachers need a strong background for understanding all of these issues and more and for refining their practices. They need at least as much knowledge of the subject to be taught as an undergraduate liberal arts major possesses. They need special knowledge in understanding how students learn concepts in a subject and what to do if students have problems learning the material. Further, teachers need considerable practice in real situations where their work is constructively criticized.

Our vision of teachers and the teaching profession requires that teacher education move beyond even the very best programs now in existence. The proposed programs include cohesive liberal education, concentrated subject specialization, and systematic study and application of pedagogy— the art, history, philosophy, and science that undergird educational processes and successful teaching.

Liberal education. All teacher education students should continue to meet at least as extensive general or liberal education requirements as other students in the college or university they attend. Liberal education should be a cohesive, planned program—not merely an accumulation of courses scattered across a number of departments. Among the courses that should be included are sociology, anthropology, and psychology, which should foster an appreciation of different cultures and heritages. Teachers also need both knowledge and understanding of literature, history, language, and the arts. All teachers need to understand the context of their world; and they must profoundly value learning, ideas, and artistic expression.

Subject specialization. The academic specialization for secondary school teachers should be in the field to be taught, and a dual major that permits teaching in two related areas may be appropriate. Every teacher at the elementary level should have an extended liberal arts program in the content areas of the elementary school, as well as specialization in child development with particular emphases on language development and thinking. Teachers should never be assigned to teach in fields for which they do not have appropriate foundations in the subject to be taught.

Professional education. Every teacher should have a strong background in professional education, because knowledge of the subject is of little consequence if the teacher cannot convey that knowledge and help students learn at a rate and level commensurate with their age and development. To accomplish the objectives of schooling, teachers need to understand how to select and present appropriate content and concepts, how to recognize the kinds of errors or difficulties students experience, and how to reteach difficult concepts. Second, they need to understand how individuals think and learn at different ages and developmental stages, how to diagnose difficulties, how to select, develop, and use appropriate teaching strategies and materials, how to observe and analyze the performance of a variety of students (including students from different cultural and ethnic backgrounds), and how to conduct discussions and seminars. Third, they need to receive systematic instruction in the organized research and experience-based information about teaching, and know how to use the knowledge being generated through research on teacher and school effectiveness. Fourth, they need to understand how technology can be integrated with effective teaching practices to ensure the development of higher-order thinking, problem solving, conceptual and social learning, rather than simple rote learning of skills. Fifth, they need to understand the conceptual relationships of the ideas and facts they learn in advanced academic courses in college to those that are appropriate to teach in elementary, middle, and high schools.

Prospective teachers also need experience teaching in real and simulated circumstances, and to have this teaching analyzed and criticized in accordance with educational science and pedagogical information that is taught in their college or university classes. Finally, they need to participate in detailed and repeated analysis and criticism of their own and others' videotaped and live teaching.

Neither formal instruction nor field work alone is sufficient preparation for the professional teacher. Quality teacher education programs do not

neither formal instruction nor field work alone is sufficient preparation for the professional teacher

12

have a mechanical separation of classwork and field experiences; instead, field work and on-campus laboratory experiences should accompany all classes, and classes or seminars should accompany all field work, such as student teaching or internships. Such programs are coherent: Early classes, laboratories, and field work anticipate what is to come, and later classes and experiences expand what came before.

Many people do not understand how teacher education programs are organized; they assume that a student's program is made up almost entirely of education courses. To the contrary, we found the following:

Only 20% of the typical program for prospective high school teachers is made up of education courses and more than a third of that is student teaching.

Approximately 40% of a teacher education student's program is made up of general liberal arts coursework, similar to that taken by students in other majors.

On the average, an additional 35% to 40% of a prospective high school teacher's program is in the field of specialization to be taught or in other liberal arts courses.

We also found that a number of efforts are underway in individual institutions and states to make significant improvements in their teacher education programs. At two institutions, for example, we noted the following:

The University of New Hampshire has had a selective, five-year teacher education program since 1975, with the following results:

40% of those accepted have become honor graduates.

Undergraduate grades average 3.1 (B) on a 4.0 scale.

Graduate Record Examination scores of those admitted to the final phase of the program averaged 1042.

The top three reasons for entering the five-year program were helping in human growth, enjoyment of children, and love of subject.

90% of those completing the program have secured teaching jobs.

13

Grambling State University, beginning in 1980, refashioned its teacher education program by aggressively recruiting high-quality students, providing tutorial programs in reading and mathematics, and totally revising the teacher education curriculum, with the following results:

85% of the students passed both the basic skills and the area specializations of the National Teachers Examination.

The number of teachers certified has increased.

Faculty members are more proud.

Faculty in arts and sciences departments are completely involved and cooperative.

Acceptance of Grambling's programs and graduates has improved.

Efforts to improve teacher education in Ohio and Georgia have been underway for ten years. More recently, Florida, Tennessee, and other states have passed legislation and provided resources for program improvements and evaluation.

Recommendations
Programs for Teacher Education

RECOMMENDATION 4: EACH TEACHER EDUCATION PROGRAM SHOULD BE AN EXACTING, INTELLECTUALLY CHALLENGING INTEGRATION OF LIBERAL STUDIES, SUBJECT SPECIALIZATION FROM WHICH SCHOOL CURRICULA ARE DRAWN, AND CONTENT AND SKILLS OF PROFESSIONAL EDUCATION.

For the programs for teacher education, the Commission's primary focus of study was the proper education of the teacher; program length and placement became issues when we identified what would be necessary for capable students to achieve such an education. * We maintain that teachers should have a liberal education equivalent to that of the best-educated members of their community, not simply a few courses in each of several general academic fields; that teachers should know and understand the intellectual and practical content from which school curricula are drawn, not simply become familiar with their portion of a school's curriculum; that teachers should have both the skills to teach and the knowledge of the research and experiential bases for those skills, not simply a set of prescriptions for what to do under various classroom circumstances.

We agreed that a program to prepare teachers must be coherent and sequential. Its intellectual demands for its students should be commensurate with the requirements of excellent teaching, not with the level of ability of the least capable student who applies for admission. Likewise only professors, supervisors, and cooperating teachers who adhere to such standards for themselves and their students should be permitted to work in the program.

Adoption of *Recommendation 4* will demand longer programs than most colleges and universities now require. (Some states already require an additional year after the baccalaureate that combines student teaching and pedagogical study.) We urge that, as states review their certification requirements and colleges and universities study their programs they let the educational needs of teachers determine the length of teacher education programs. We particularly encourage those colleges and universities offering only a baccalaureate degree and those having graduate programs to explore mutually beneficial arrangements that will permit all highly qualified students desiring to become teachers to complete the best program possible.

---

*The members of the Commission whose names appear below support the recommendations contained in this report but are concerned that some of the recommendations are not far reaching enough. We are concerned particularly about the issues of the liberal education prospective teachers should receive and about the amount of time needed to properly prepare teachers for the future.

First, we contend that one cannot be liberally educated without in-depth study in at least one academic subject. All prospective teachers, as part of their liberal education, should be educated in at least one academic major. This is as true for the person who will teach first grade as it is for the person who will teach high school physics.

Second, we believe that the kind of teacher education program proposed by the Commission cannot take place within the usual four-year baccalaureate. A minimum of four years should be devoted to the liberal arts component of the teacher education program; a minimum of five years to the total program

American education would be strengthened if the Commission had been more forthright on these issues.

J. Myron Atkin
John E. Brown
Stephen Cobb
Mary Harwood Futrell
Jonathan C Messerli
Howard C. Nielson
Albert Shanker
Mark Shibles
Richard C. Wallace, Jr.

15

RECOMMENDATION 5: FOLLOWING THEIR COMPLETION OF A TEACHER EDUCATION PROGRAM AND THE AWARDING OF A PROVISIONAL CERTIFICATE, NEW TEACHERS SHOULD COMPLETE AN INDUCTION PERIOD OR INTERNSHIP OF AT LEAST A YEAR'S DURATION FOR WHICH COMPENSATION IS PROVIDED.

We advise all states to develop for teacher candidates an internship or other induction experience beyond the provisional certification requirement. During this period, the school, the profession, and higher education should work together to help the new teacher become successfully immersed in the teaching profession. Because the provisionally certified teachers will render real teaching services, compensation is justified much as it is in other professions that require internships. Interns, however, should have reduced teaching loads so that they have time to participate in professional development activites, including seminars.

RECOMMENDATION 6: STATES SHOULD ENCOURAGE AND ASSIST THE DEVELOPMENT AND EVALUATION OF EXPERIMENTAL TEACHER EDUCATION PROGRAMS.

In considering experimental programs, we urge that states provide resources and support to colleges and universities that want to design, test, and evaluate new approaches in teacher education. Colleges and universities should be encouraged to consider major structural changes, not just course modification; and states should be willing to adjust existing regulations, with appropriate monitoring, to test the new models. In particular, states should assist colleges and universities to form consortia that build on the strengths of the various constituent members.

Accountability
for Teacher Education

Control over teacher education is too scattered: Colleges and universities decide whether to establish teacher education programs and states decide whether to permit them to do so. Each state sets its own standards for teacher education programs and for the certification of teachers; each college or university decides how it will meet those standards and, after its programs receive state approval, whether to apply for national voluntary accreditation. We found the following:

More than 1,200 colleges and universities have teacher education programs. This number increased by 100 in the 1970s when the need for teachers was dropping.

Of the colleges and universities having teacher education programs, 45% offer only baccalaureate degrees, 42% also offer a master degree, and 14% offer the doctorate.

Essentially, all teacher education programs have state approval; fewer than 45% have national accreditation; the percentage varies widely among states and regions and among types of institutions.

The diffusion of responsibility for teacher education is perhaps its greatest source of vigor, as it permits experimentation with different kinds of programs. Conversely, diffusion is a source of trouble, because it permits too many mediocre and substandard programs to exist. The findings below support our conclusion that the process needs more order:

There is relatively little coordination among the states for setting approval and certification standards and processes, and a similar lack of

17

coordination between state approval processes and voluntary national accreditation.

Between 1979 and 1984, the National Council for Accreditation of Teacher Education denied accreditation to one or more programs in 15% of the colleges and universities that it reviewed. All of these programs had previously received state approval.

The challenges of classrooms and schools, combined with political and economic factors that affect schools, require teachers with a strong professional sense of what they are doing and how they can grow in their profession. Yet, some states have introduced alternative teacher preparation programs that do not include systematic attention to professional knowledge and skill. Some alternative programs are essentially apprenticeships. In an apprenticeship, a novice learns by watching how a skilled artisan does the job and then imitating that performance. We do not believe that imitative training alone can produce a professional of the caliber needed in this nation's classrooms, and we advise states to reconsider approving such programs.

Recommendations
Accountability for Teacher Education

RECOMMENDATION 7: CERTIFICATION AND PROGRAM APPROVAL STANDARDS AND DECISIONS SHOULD CONTINUE TO BE STATE RESPONSIBILITIES IN CONSULTATION WITH THE PROFESSION.

We recognize that approval to teach is a state responsibility no matter how the state decides to exercise that responsibility. We urge, however, that states delegate major responsibility to educational professionals for assuring that high standards are set and met by those who prepare teachers and those who seek a state's license to teach.

States should insist on adherence to their certification processes. A state should not permit teacher candidates to circumvent the process—that is, for example, state certification is based on approval of teacher education programs, and a candidate should not be certified on the basis of a list of courses taken in another state when those courses do not meet the state's standards. States also should not issue emergency certificates if the candidates do not meet standards.

We endorse the concept of peer review and recommendation in the licensing process, either by a professional practices board or some other carefully designed procedure that assures adequate professional participation. We applaud the actions of several states in making license renewal more rigorous. We also recognize that, because education is primarily a tax-supported enterprise in which government mandates attendance and often assigns the student both to the building and to the teacher, the state carries the burden of assuring quality services. The state's responsibility for quality, we believe, should be acknowledged in standards for teacher certification and recertification as well as in support for the schools.

RECOMMENDATION 8: STATES SHOULD MAINTAIN AND STRICTLY ENFORCE RIGOROUS STANDARDS FOR PROGRAM REVIEW. VOLUNTARY NATIONAL ACCREDITATION SHOULD BE STRENGTHENED AND MADE TO SERVE AS A MEANS FOR IMPROVING TEACHER EDUCATION.

All states except one now give formal approval to colleges and universities to offer programs for teacher preparation. Approval is granted subject to periodic review and compliance with a set of program standards. The profession should be active in assuring that high standards for program approval are established and maintained.

This recommendation for strengthening the standards for program approval is not a plea for more detail. Quite the contrary, in many instances reduction of detail may be more desirable. Our recommendation is for programs that are more selective; courses that are intellectually more demanding and more closely tied to the expanding research base; and supervision that is more frequent, more explicit in its expectations, more rigorous, and more cooperative.

the recommendation for strengthening the standards for program approval is not a plea for more detail

National accreditation in the past was intended both to provide a basis for certification reciprocity and to help improve teacher education. Numerous reciprocity agreements are now in place and others are being negotiated, thus largely obviating the need for additional assistance with this function; however, national voluntary accreditation remains a potential for improving teacher education in the same manner that it serves numerous other professions, such as engineering, architecture, nursing, law, and dentistry.

We encourage the continued setting of higher standards for granting program accreditation.

RECOMMENDATION 9: TEACHER EDUCATION PROGRAMS SHOULD CONTINUE TO BE LOCATED IN COLLEGES AND UNIVERSITIES.

A few states, because of concerns about shortages of teachers to fill immediate needs, are taking steps to remove teacher education from colleges and universities and to adopt what are apprenticeship programs. We consider this a serious mistake, and we strongly oppose such alternative programs. Apprenticeship models do not allow for the systematic, integrated study of content and pedagogy essential to the preparation of teachers. Teachers need teacher education programs in which they develop mastery of their subject, principles of teaching and learning, and teaching skills.

We encourage the formation of teacher education programs for older students. These special programs should provide these prospective teachers with opportunities to update their knowledge of their subject specialization while they primarily study the principles and processes of teaching. Alternative programs should assure the same competencies as those designed for traditional college students. The fundamental differences between an alternative and a traditional program are the audience and the training design, not the content, the rigor, or the expected outcomes.

Resources
for Teacher Education

Teacher education has been treated as a low-cost program in colleges and universities. It has not received, for example, necessary resources to recruit students or to provide scholarships and loans to even its best students; and frequently it has not received the essential funds for providing even minimal equipment and clinical supervision. In addition, teacher education has received only limited amounts of support for research and for the development and dissemination of research information and products; and it has had almost no funding for postgraduate preparation of potential leaders in teacher education. State and federal governments as well as colleges, universities, and private foundations must accept responsibility for the proper funding of teacher education if the essential advances are to be made.

Programs to prepare teachers are typically funded on the same basis as liberal arts lecture courses. At least three factors cause teacher education programs to require special funding beyond that for traditional lecture courses: (1) At each step of laboratory and field experience, a teacher candidate must have individual supervision and guidance. (2) Specialized equipment is needed, such as video machines for analysis and critique of a candidate's performance in campus clinical settings and in schools, microcomputers for instructing students how to use technology in both simple and complex learning tasks, and laboratories for producing and using slides, transparencies, and other teaching aids. (3) The faculty required in quality teacher education programs, faculty who have skills and experience in teaching, research, and supervision, are in high demand in other positions. Incentives are needed to attract and keep such faculty in teacher education. For these reasons, supporting teacher education on the same basis as liberal arts lecture courses is simply inadequate. We heard the following:

Data from a major state university show that twice as much money is spent on educating an engineer as a teacher and almost 60% more on educating a business graduate.

At the University of New Hampshire, teacher education's most serious problem is the lack of financial support for its extended program.

Progress in any profession depends on the information and products of research and development. During the past fifteen years educational research and development have produced a substantial amount of useful information on the use of instructional time, procedures for instruction, management of classes, teacher planning, higher-order thought processes, reading comprehension, and the long-term value of preschool education. Research and development cost money, however, and needed research has been badly neglected in recent years because of reduced funding. Many serious problems have gone unsolved, in great part because the research is so limited. Further, restricted funding and the absence of sophisticated means of dissemination have hindered the widespread use of the research information that has been produced. On the need for research support, we found the following:

Illiteracy is considered a threat to the nation's welfare and, for the person who cannot read, a tragedy equivalent to a severe physical impairment. Yet, the U.S. Department of Education probably spends less than three million dollars per year on reading research.

The total federal share of the budget for K-12 education in the United States was approximately $9.5 billion in 1983–84. Federal expenditure for educational research and development is less than $100 million, or approximately one percent of the federal share of the K-12 operating budget.

Until recently, relatively little effort was made to ensure the inclusion of new research findings in teacher education programs. Efforts at inclusion are still fragmentary.

A positive step has been taken in Florida, where a full-year induction period has been built around research information now available.

Major improvements in teacher education will require faculty who not only are skilled in their particular fields of expertise, but also have a broad

restricted funding and an absence of sophisticated means of dissemination have hindered the widespread use of research

22

understanding of the process of teacher education. Faculty should be able to contribute to the development of teacher education programs that are cohesive and integrated and that incorporate field experience with academic coursework. They should be able to model the best teaching and foster problem-solving and critical-thinking skills. They also should hold high standards for their students, standards that are based on an accurate perception of the complex demands of teaching.

Few doctoral degree programs prepare aspiring teacher education faculty for such roles; in addition, few formal opportunities exist for current faculty to expand their expertise in these areas. If teacher education is to make major structural changes and program improvements, resources must be allocated for the professional development of the faculty responsible for making those changes.

Recommendations
Resources for Teacher Education

RECOMMENDATION 10: SUFFICIENT RESOURCES MUST BE ASSIGNED TO TEACHER EDUCATION TO PROVIDE THOROUGH, RIGOROUS PROGRAMS.

A not-so-benign neglect has contributed to the problems in teacher education; significantly increased support by responsible leaders and policymakers is needed if it is to improve. Teacher education must become an all-campus priority, and presidential leadership is the only way to achieve this. We urge college and university presidents to carefully and thoroughly evaluate their teacher education programs and those who are graduated from them. If programs are less than first rate, they should either be given the resources and leadership to make them so, or they should be closed.

RECOMMENDATION 11: FEDERAL AND STATE GOVERNMENTS SHOULD PROVIDE SUPPORT AND ENCOURAGEMENT FOR THE FURTHER DEVELOPMENT, DISSEMINATION, AND USE OF RESEARCH INFORMATION IN EDUCATION AND TEACHER EDUCATION.

No business, industry, or profession could develop properly with the level of expenditure that currently is allocated to educational research and

23

development. To supply the funds necessary for increased efforts in educational research, we urge the federal government to increase its financial commitment to educational research, and the states to fund or to increase their support for programs of educational research and development.

RECOMMENDATION 12: A NATIONAL ACADEMY FOR TEACHER EDUCATION SHOULD BE ESTABLISHED, TO WHICH PROMISING TEACHER EDUCATORS COULD BE NOMINATED FOR POSTGRADUATE TRAINEESHIPS.

We advocate that a National Academy for Teacher Education be created, and that it be supported by a combination of corporate and institutional memberships. A National Academy would provide visible national leadership for faculty development and program improvement, and would provide individual faculty, particularly those early in their careers, with opportunities not usually available within their institutions. The Academy's membership would include teacher educators from college campuses as well as their colleagues from the schools, who have responsibilities for preparing teachers.

A National Academy would have symbolic and functional value. Symbolically, it would give recognition that the nation values the preparation of its teachers. Functionally, it would provide postgraduate preparation to a substantial corps of teacher educators. By bringing together diverse groups to share their different experiences in a variety of courses and seminars and by providing these gifted teacher educators with common experiences, they would be better prepared to assist in improving teacher education throughout the United States.

Conditions Necessary to Support the Highest Quality Teaching

Most of this report's recommendations are about recruiting talented people who want to be teachers and training them in programs that are more selective and more demanding. Such recommendations for more stringent qualifications and training, however, presuppose that fundamental changes will be made in the working conditions in America's schools. Current conditions in schools work against lifelong commitment to teaching as a career.

Inadequate salaries, limited advancement opportunities, stressful work environments, and lack of status and autonomy discourage many of the best students from ever considering careers in teaching. The same factors prompt many teachers to leave the profession after a few years, often when their skills are highly developed and their potential contributions are the greatest. One of the nation's more difficult challenges is to find ways to make the work environment and reward structure consistent with the caliber of teaching service that children need and parents demand. We call your attention to the following:

In 1981, in response to, "If you could go back and start all over again, would you still become a teacher?" almost 40% of the respondents said, "No." This rate of dissatisfaction was four times higher than teachers indicated twenty years ago.

The level of dissatisfaction among secondary school teachers was significantly higher than among their elementary school colleagues. The percent of secondary teachers expressing dissatisfaction with salaries was twice as high (50% versus 25%); the percent expressing dissatisfaction with administrative support was ten times as high (40% versus 4%).

Although teachers' salaries increased from 1971 to 1981, inflation ac-

tually decreased their paychecks almost 15%. Because this kind of decline was not experienced by others, it further reduced the attractiveness of teaching as a career.

Salary increases tend to be concentrated in the first third of a teacher's career, which means that for the last twenty-five to thirty years, salary increases do not serve as significant motivators.

87% of teachers leaving the profession cited inadequate salaries as a factor in their resignations. Of almost equal importance was the universal perception that society did not highly value the contribution they were making. "It's the only job in the world," said one teacher, "in which you read in the paper in the morning what an awful job you are doing."

Kansas teachers leaving the profession gave salary as the most important reason for leaving, classroom conditions as second, and lack of administrative support as third.

Recommendations
Conditions Necessary to Support
the Highest Quality Teaching

RECOMMENDATION 13: TEACHERS' SALARIES SHOULD BE INCREASED AT THE BEGINNING OF AND THROUGHOUT THEIR CAREERS TO LEVELS COMMENSURATE WITH OTHER PROFESSIONS REQUIRING COMPARABLE TRAINING AND EXPERTISE.

We urge state and local governing boards and others who are responsible for compensating teachers to take vigorous and immediate action to improve teachers' salaries both at the beginning of and throughout their careers. Increased pay, combined with opportunities for advancement within the profession and incentives for exceptional performance, can do much to stem the exodus of highly qualified teachers into school administration or private enterprise where rewards are more attractive. Significantly improved salaries, more than any other single action, will encourage talented, highly qualified students to become teachers.

We hold that four concepts should guide discussions and decisions on teachers' salaries: (1) The beginning salary should be equivalent to that for

26

other professions that require comparable schooling and expertise. (2) Additional compensation for all teachers who demonstrate high competence in various roles, as judged according to valid, equitable evaluation systems, should be available throughout a teacher's career without forcing him or her to leave the classroom. (3) Incentives should be available to help individual teachers improve their capacity to teach. Incentives might include college or university programs, ongoing staff development during the school day, sabbatical leaves, travel, and opportunities to participate in career ladders, and to advance within the teaching profession. (4) In addition to incentives for individual teachers, other incentives should be available to help schools increase their capacity to serve through improved faculty assignments. For instance, teachers might work with the induction of new teachers, in development of curricula, on peer review panels, in cooperative research and development projects, and in different time assignments such as a ten- or eleven-month school year or a part-time assignment.

Incentives to pursue additional college or university work should be maintained, but careful scrutiny of the quality and content of courses and programs is recommended.

RECOMMENDATION 14: TEACHERS' RESPONSIBILITIES AND WORKING CONDITIONS SHOULD BE COMMENSURATE WITH THE REQUIREMENTS OF THE JOB.

Teachers have limited autonomy and decision-making authority to produce the kinds of services that students need. Beyond the absence of rights to make the decisions they are most qualified to make, teachers also do not have telephones, offices, or direct secretarial assistance. Sometimes, they do not even have sufficient books, paper, or chalk, not to mention the technology now available in most work places. They enjoy little time to plan and even less time to grade assignments or give personal instruction. They are often expected to collect lunch money, monitor halls, and plan pep rallies—circumstances that waste the teacher's value and deter attracting and maintaining quality teachers.

We urge state and local school boards and others who are responsible for the work environment in schools to examine the physical and professional circumstances in which teachers work. These circumstances should

teachers have limited autonomy and decision-making authority to produce the kinds of services that students need be judged not only by past practices in schools, but also by the standards used in other professions requiring similar education and expertise. Teaching must be viewed as a teacher's primary responsibility; other activities should be assigned to qualified support personnel. Teachers' participation in making decisions for their schools also should be expanded, and the overall teaching conditions should be significantly improved.

These changes should not be viewed primarily as benefits to the teachers, although they will profit from the changes, but rather as benefits to the school system and its students. Economically, it is inefficient to use the time and efforts of highly trained, highly productive professionals to do work that can be handled by paraprofessionals having less expensive training. Professional should perform the tasks for which they are trained and then be held to the highest performance standards.

RECOMMENDATION 15: TEACHERS SHOULD BE PROVIDED PROFESSIONAL DEVELOPMENT OPPORTUNITIES AND INCENTIVES SO THAT THEY CAN CONSISTENTLY IMPROVE THEIR PRACTICE.

Local school boards must provide opportunities for teachers to experience success in teaching and to fully develop their professional competence. Teachers should be given assignments for which they are qualified, appropriate class loads, and support services.

State boards of education should set as their top priority for 1985 the improvement of the professional development of teachers. The federal government and local school boards must also recognize their responsibility for the continuing development of educational professionals; teachers must continue to enhance their skills if they are to teach youngsters effectively and provide the leadership required to meet the challenges of excellence and equity. Staff development programs that go beyond expanding awareness to achieving competence should be promoted on a local or, where schools are small, a regional basis. We also urge that state boards of education extend the requirements for recertification of teachers to include competency-based professional development that is evaluated locally.

We recommend that staff development programs be based on research findings. Research suggests that teachers should have opportunities to try

state boards of education should set as their top priority for 1985 the improvement of the professional development of teachers

28

out new skills in simulated settings and receive feedback and follow-up coaching to ensure that their application leads to effective instruction. Research indicates that staff development activities should be designed and conducted to help teachers build upon skills developed during their teacher education programs and during induction. Staff development activities should provide opportunities for teachers to interact with each other, again according to research, and they should relate to opportunities for career development in collaboration with graduate schools of education

We encourage federal and state governments to provide funds for evaluating staff development programs. The profession needs evaluation research to clarify the effects of staff development. Federal and state agencies should require impact evaluation studies on the ultimate beneficiaries of staff development programs, namely, the children and the schools. These impact studies should be program, not individual, evaluations.

RECOMMENDATION 16: ADMINISTRATOR PREPARATION SHOULD BE EXTENDED, FOCUSING ON INSTRUCTIONAL LEADERSHIP AND ON THE CREATION OF CONDITIONS FOR PROFESSIONAL PRACTICE FOR TEACHERS.

We urge state and local education agencies to recognize that building principals and superintendents, more than any other individuals, are responsible for developing and promoting the environment for the professional growth of teachers and for establishing a collegial environment in which teachers are viewed as partners in efforts to improve instruction. We urge that administrative training programs in higher education be examined and modified to provide for explicit educational leadership skills in existing and potential administrators.

We further urge local education agencies to recognize that building principals will have to delegate some managerial duties in order to assume the leadership role we propose. Building principals may need additional personnel to assist in managing their schools, so that they have time to provide educational leadership.

Our Call for Change

To secure the future of the nation's children, a new generation of teachers is needed, teachers who are

competent in their subjects,

skilled in teaching,

informed about children and their development,

knowledgeable about cognitive psychology,

schooled in technology,

informed about the latest, most relevant research,

able to work with peers and others in diverse environments, and

confident of their roles and contributions.

To secure the future of the nation's teachers, a new generation of teacher education programs is essential, programs that are vigorous, exciting, and comprehensive in all the elements that give a woman or man the basis for becoming a great teacher.

If we are to secure the future for America's dreams and aspirations, a nationwide commitment to excellent teacher education and to super, exciting schools is imperative.

References

Applied Systems Institute. (1984). *Tomorrow's teachers* (Contract No. 300-83-0160). Washington, DC: National Institute of Education.

Association for School, College and University Staffing. (1984). *Teacher supply/demand 1984*. Madison, WI: Author.

Association for School, College and University Staffing. (1985). *Teacher supply/demand 1985*. Madison, WI: Author.

Andrew, M. D. (1983). The characteristics of students in a five-year teacher education program. *Journal of Teacher Education*, *34*(1), 20-23.

Andrew, M.D. (1984). *Restructuring teacher education: The University of New Hampshire's five year program*. Durham, NH: University of New Hampshire. (Indexed in March 1985 issue of ERIC Resources in Education.)

Bull, B. (1984). *Council of Postsecondary Education report on teacher education*. Olympia, Washington: Council of Postsecondary Education.

Cyphert, F., & Nichelson, J. E. (1984). *Teacher education redesign in Ohio: Past, present and future*. Columbus, OH: Ohio State University. (Indexed in March 1985 issue of ERIC *Resources in Education*)

Kansas Committee on Why Teachers Leave Teaching. (1983). Topeka, KS: Kansas State Department of Education.

Kluender, M. M., & Egbert, R. L. (1983). *The status of American teacher education*. Draft report to the National Institute of Education.

Leach, J.W., & Solomon, L. (1984). *Performance-based certification in Georgia: Present and future*. Atlanta, GA: Georgia State Department of Education. (Indexed in March 1985 issue of ERIC *Resources in Education*)

National Center for Educational Statistics. (1980). *The condition of education 1980 edition*. Washington, DC: U.S. Government Printing Office.

National Center for Educational Statistics. (1983). *The condition of education 1983 edition*. Washington, DC: U.S. Government Printing Office.

National Center for Educational Statistics. (1984). *The condition of education 1984 edition*. Washington, DC: U.S. Government Printing Office.

National Center for Health Statistics. (1958-1984). *Natality reports*. Washington, DC: U.S. Government Printing Office.

National Education Association. (1982). *Teacher supply and demand in public schools, 1980-81*. Washington, DC: National Education Association.

Saunders, R. L. (1984). *Efforts to reform teacher education in Tennessee: A ten-year analysis*. Memphis, TN: Memphis State University. (Indexed in March 1985 issue of ERIC *Resources in Education*)

Schlechty, P. C., & Vance, V. S. (1983). Recruitment, selection and retention: The shape of the teaching force. *Elementary School Journal*, *83*(4), 469-487.

Smith, D. C., & Wilson, G. W. (1984). *The Florida beginning teacher program*. Gainesville, FL: University of Florida. (Indexed in March 1985 issue of ERIC *Resources in Education*)

Smith, G. P. (in press). The impact of competency tests on teacher education: Ethical and legal issues in selecting and certifying teachers. In M. Haberman (Ed.), *Research in teacher education*. Norwood, NJ: ABLEX.

U.S. Bureau of the Census. (1984). *Current population reports* Series P-25, #952. Washington, DC: U.S. Government Printing Office.

Vance, V. S., & Schlechty, P. C. (1982). The distribution of academic ability in the teaching force: Policy implication. *Phi Delta Kappan*, *64*(1), 22-27.

Weaver, W. T. (1981). The alent pool in teacher education. *Journal of Teacher Education*, *32*(3), 32-36.

APPENDICES

APPENDIX A: Biographical Sketches of Commission Members

J. Myron Atkin   has been Dean of the School of Education at Stanford University since 1979, a position he assumed after serving as Dean of the College of Education at the University of Illinois for ten years. His specializations are the teaching of science and the evaluation of educational programs. His recent writings focus on institutional change and the relationship between research and improvement of educational practice.

Frank B. Brouillet   has served as Superintendent of Public Instruction in the State of Washington since 1973, and as President of the Council of Chief State School Officers in 1984. Dr. Brouillet is a member of the Board of Directors of the Northwest Regional Educational Laboratory, and the Washington State Council for Postsecondary Education. Prior to becoming superintendent, Dr. Brouillet was a member of the Washington State House of Representatives from 1956 to 1972, where he chaired the House Education Committee and the Joint House-Senate Committee on Education.

John E. Brown   is President of Coe College in Cedar Rapids, Iowa. Educated at the University of Kansas and Stanford University, he has taught history at both universities, and at Lewis and Clark College, where he was also Vice President for Academic Affairs and Provost. Dr. Brown has served as a consultant to the Danforth Foundation; the U.S. Department of Health, Education, and Welfare; and as Chairman of the Oregon Committee for the Humanities. His honors include election to Phi Beta Kappa, selection as a Woodrow Wilson Fellow and Woodrow Wilson Dissertation Fellow, and inclusion in *Who's Who in America*.

Stephen Cobb   has been a member of the Tennessee General Assembly since 1974. Representative Cobb was educated at Harvard, A.B. 1966, and Vanderbilt, M.A., Ph.D. (Sociology), and

J.D. In 1977–78 he was a Fulbright scholar to France where he lectured on political science, sociology, and law at the University of Caen. In the General Assembly, he serves as Chair of the Education Oversight Committee and Secretary of the Finance, Ways and Means Committee. A Democrat, he was the initial sponsor of Tennessee's Master Teacher program.

Mary Hatwood Futrell

a classroom teacher in Alexandria, Virginia, is President of the National Education Association. Her NEA experience spans a wide spectrum of service to the organization and the profession, including work with state agencies and with the National Council for Accreditation of Teacher Education. Ms. Futrell was honored by the American Association of Colleges for Teacher Education in 1984 when she delivered the annual Charles W. Hunt Lecture at the Association's convention. She has represented the nation's teachers in major magazines and on all of the top television "talk shows." *Ms.* magazine named her one of its ten "Women of the Year" for 1984.

Robert D. Graham

Governor of Florida, is serving his second term as governor of America's fastest growing urban state. His priorities as governor have centered on improving the quality of the state's public education system, which he considers a tool to strengthen the economy and raise the quality of life. Governor Graham has led the movement to reform the public schools through a broad-based strategy of raising standards and classroom performance to generate public support for greater resources for education.

Mari-Luci Jaramillo

Associate Dean for the College of Education at the University of New Mexico, served from 1980 to 1982 as a special assistant to the President of the University of New Mexico. From 1977 to 1980, she interrupted her twenty years of teaching and administration at the university to serve as U.S. Ambassador to Honduras. She has extensive experience in the areas of bilingual education, multicultural education, teacher education, school curriculum and methodology, civil and minority rights, and international education and diplomacy.

C. Peter Magrath

(pronounced Ma-grah), the Commission's Chairperson, became President of the University of Missouri system on January 1. For the past ten years, Dr. Magrath was President of the University of Minnesota, and from 1972 to 1974, as president of the State University of New York at Binghamton. After receiving his Ph.D. in political science from Cornell University, he began his career at Brown University, followed by the University of Nebraska-Lincoln. Dr. Magrath has served on a variety of national boards, and he is the current chair of the National Association of State Universities and Land-Grant Colleges, and the current Vice Chair of the Association of American Universities. *Time* magazine listed Dr. Magrath among its "200 Leaders for the Future," and *Change* magazine included him among the "100 Leaders in American Higher Education."

Jonathan C. Messerli

is President of Muhlenberg College in Allentown, Pennsylvania. He served as President of Susquehanna University and Dean at the Schools of Education at Hofstra and Fordham Universities, after having taught at Columbia Teachers College and the University of Washington. He holds a Ph.D. from Harvard University, and is the author of *Horace Mann, A Biography* (Knopf, 1972) and numerous articles on higher education.

Howard C. Nielson

was elected to the U.S. House of Representatives from Utah in 1982, after serving in the Utah House of Representatives for four terms, including one as Majority Leader and one as Speaker. Congressman Nielson holds an M.S. from the University of Oregon, and an M.B.A. and a Ph.D. from Stanford University. He has worked in private enterprise as a statistician and research economist, and has taught business administration and statistics at Brigham Young University. He also served as Associate Commissioner of Higher Education in Utah. Congressman Nielson is a member of the House Education and Labor Committee and also of the House Energy and Commerce Committee.

M. Joan Parent

is Immediate Past President of the National School Boards Association. She is also Past President of the Minnesota School Boards Association and the Minnesota State High School League. She was a member of the Forum of Educational Organization Leaders for two years, and has served on the National Science Board's Commission on Pre-College Education in Mathematics, Science and Technology, and on the Education Commission of the States' Commission for Excellence. Dr. Parent, who is a retired veterinarian, earned her degree from the University of Guelph in Guelph, Ontario, Canada.

W. Ann Reynolds is Chief Executive Officer of California State University, the nation's largest system of four-year and graduate-level higher education institutions, with 19 campuses, more than 316,000 students, and 35,000 faculty and staff. Dr. Reynolds was Provost of Ohio State University, and has served as Associate Vice Chancellor for research and Dean of the Graduate College at the University of Illinois Medical Center. Dr. Reynolds, an award-winning scholar in developmental biology, specializes in studies of fetal development, placental transfer, and nutrition. She is the author or co-author of more than 100 scholarly works.

J. T. Sandefur is Dean of the College of Education, Western Kentucky University. He is serving at present as the Chairman of the National Council for Accreditation of Teacher Education. He is a Past President of the American Association of Colleges for Teacher Education, Past President of the Teacher Education Council of State Colleges and Universities, and current Chair of the National Advisory Board of the Research and Development Center for Teacher Education at the University of Texas, Austin.

Sister Michelle Schiffgens Ph.D., is Chair of the Division of Education/Physical Education/Psychology at Marycrest College in Davenport, Iowa. She served on the Board of Directors of the American Association of Colleges for Teacher Education from 1975 to 1979, and as President of the Association of Independent Liberal Arts Colleges for Teacher Education during 1981–82. Her areas of specialization are curriculum and instruction, administration, and reading disabilities.

Albert Shanker has been president of the American Federation of Teachers, AFL-CIO, since 1974. Mr. Shanker also sits on the AFL-CIO Executive Council and is president of AFT's New York

40

City local, the United Federation of Teachers. He has been secretary of the Jewish Labor Committee, and serves on several Boards, including the A. Philip Randolph Institute, the League for Industrial Democracy, and the International Rescue Committee. He has appeared on nationally broadcast news and public affairs programs, and writes a weekly column on education, labor, and human rights issues.

Mark Shibles   is Dean of the School of Education at the University of Connecticut. He received his Ph.D. from Cornell University in 1968. Dr. Shibles has been a consultant to state education departments, school districts, and colleges and universities. He has served on the Board of Directors of the American Association of Colleges for Teacher Education and was Chair of its Governmental Relations Commission. Dr. Shibles is President-elect of the Association of Colleges and Schools of Education in State Universities and Land-Grant Colleges and Affiliated Private Universities.

Richard C. Wallace, Jr.   is Superintendent of Schools in Pittsburgh, Pennsylvania. Pittsburgh is recognized for its vigorous staff development programs. The Schenley High School Teacher Center reflects the District's intense commitment to revitalize its secondary school teachers. An elementary Teacher Center will open in September 1985. Dr. Wallace has a strong interest in developing instructional leadership skills in Administrators. He is an adjunct Professor in educational administration at the University of Pittsburgh.

APPENDIX B: Schedule of the Commission's Public Events

Event	Host(s)
Commission Meeting May 2, 1984 Chicago, IL	
Hearing September 25–26, 1984 University of Minnesota Minneapolis, MN	William Gardner, Dean Kenneth Howey, Associate Dean College of Education University of Minnesota
Hearing October 4–5, 1984 University of Texas Austin, TX	Gene Hall, Director Frank Gonzales Research and Development Center University of Texas at Austin
Hearing October 15–16, 1984 Georgia State University Atlanta, GA	Jerry Robbins, Dean Janet Towslee-Collier, Associate Dean College of Education Georgia State University
Hearing October `18–19, 1984 New York University New York, NY	Robert Burnham, Dean Theodore Repa, Professor School of Education New York University
Hearing October 22–23, 1984 San Francisco State University San Francisco, CA	Henrietta Schwartz, Dean College of Education San Francisco State University
Commission Meeting December 3, 1984 Chicago, IL	
Commission Meeting January 15, 1985 St. Louis, MO	

APPENDIX C: Seminar Themes and Related Activities

Hearing Site	Seminar Theme	Related Activities
Minneapolis	Research and Teacher Education	Discussion with teacher educators from University of Minnesota and College of Saint Catherine
Austin	Teacher Education and the Schools	Participation in Conference "Beyond the Looking Glass" Site visits to: • Saint Edwards University • University of Texas at Austin
Atlanta	The State's Responsibility for Teacher Education	Breakfast with Atlanta School District and Atlanta region teacher education leaders Site visits to: • Atlanta University • Georgia State University
New York	The Implications for Teacher Education of Radically Different Assumptions about Schools	Visit with New York University NCATE team
San Francisco	Higher Education's Responsibility for Teacher Education	Site visits to: • Mills College • Stanford University • San Francisco State University

APPENDIX D: Commissioned Papers

Author(s)	Paper
Michael D. Andrew University of New Hampshire	"Restructuring Teacher Education: The University of New Hampshire's Five Year Program"
Herman E. Behling, Jr. Maryland State Department of Education	"Quality Control of Teacher Preparation Programs Through the Program Approval Process"
Ken Carlson Rutgers University	"The Teacher Certification Struggle—New Jersey"
Frederick R. Cyphert The Ohio State University John E. Nichelson Ohio Department of Education	"Teacher Education Redesign in Ohio: Past, Present and Future"
Barbara Dubitsky Bank Street College of Education	"The Implications for Teacher Education of Assuming that Schools of the Future Will Have Unlimited Access to Technology"
David H. Florio American Federation of Teachers	"Excellence in Teacher Education, Options for a Federal Partnership"
Eva Galambos Southern Regional Education Board	"Testing Teachers for Certification and Re-Certification"
Hendrik D. Gideonse University of Cincinnati	"Guiding Images for Teaching and Teacher Education"
Gary A. Griffin University of Illinois/Chicago	"Crossing the Bridge: The First Years of Teaching"
Martin Haberman University of Wisconsin—Milwaukee	"An Evaluation of the Rationale for Required Teacher Education: Beginning Teachers With and Without Teacher Preparation"
Gene Hall Research and Development Center for Teacher Education University of Texas at Austin	"The Schools and Preservice Education: Expectations and Reasonable Solutions"

44

Author(s)	Paper
Kenneth R. Howey University of Minnesota	"The Next Generation of Teacher Preparation Programs"
Linda Bunnell Jones The California State University System	"Teacher Education: An All-University Concept"
Harry Judge Oxford University	"Teacher Education in Other (Non-U.S.) Countries"
Mary Kluender University of Nebraska—Lincoln	"The Nebraska Consortium for the Improvement of Teacher Education"
Richard C. Kunkel National Council for Accreditation of Teacher Education	"The Place and Appropriate Future of National Accreditation"
J. William Leach Lester Solomon Georgia State Department of Education	"Performance-Based Certification in Georgia: Present and Future"
Edward J. Meade, Jr. The Ford Foundation	"Recent Reports on Education: Some Implications for Preparing Teachers"
Norma Nutter University of Northern Colorado	"Resources Needed for an Excellent Teacher Preparation Program"
Bruce A. Peseau University of Alabama	"Resources Allocated to Teacher Education in State Universities and Land-Grant Colleges"
Marilyn Rauth American Federation of Teachers	"Testing for Certification and Recertification"
Mary Anne Raywid Hofstra University	"Preparing Teachers for Schools of Choice"
Sharon P. Robinson National Education Association	"Toward a More Desirable Profession"
Robert L. Saunders Memphis State University	"Efforts to Reform Teacher Education in Tennessee: A Ten-Year Analysis"

Author(s)	Paper
Dale Scannell University of Kansas	"The University of Kansas Extended Teacher Education Program"
Phillip Schlechty University of North Carolina— Chapel Hill	"Schools with Career Ladders or Differentiated Staffing"
Henrietta Schwartz San Francisco State University	"Recruitment, Selection, Retention and Graduation of Teacher Education Candidates"
B. Othanel Smith University of South Florida	"Research Bases for Teacher Education"
David C. Smith University of Florida	"Proteach: An Extended Preservice Teacher Preparation Program"
David C. Smith University of Florida Garfield Wilson Florida Department of Education	"The Florida Beginning Teacher Program"
Richard C. Wallace, Jr. Superintendent of Schools Pittsburgh Public Schools	"Post-Certification Development of Teachers and Administrators"

APPENDIX E: Testimony Presented at Hearings

Minneapolis, Minnesota

Presenter	Title of Testimony
Ruth Randall Minnesota Commissioner of Education	
Marti Zins Minnesota Education Association	
Kenneth Peatross Minnesota Board of Teaching	
Ross Nielsen University of Northern Iowa	

Robert Gabrick
St. Croix Valley Association of
  Teacher Educators
	"History of the St. Croix Valley
	  Association of Teacher Educators"

John R. McClellan
Minnesota Association of School
  Administrators
	"Research and Teacher Education as
	  Viewed by the MASA"

Austin, Texas

Presenter	Title of Testimony

Richard Swain
Texas Association of Secondary School
  Principals
	"The Neglected Obligation of the
	  Teaching Profession"

Ben M. Harris The University of Texas at Austin	"Instructional Supervision for Excellence in Education"
G. Pritchy Smith Jarvis Christian College	"Competency Testing: Excellence Without Equity"

47

Presenter	Title of Testimony
Lowell J. Bethel The University of Texas at Austin	"The College of Education and Field-Based Experiences in a Teacher Education Program"
Ernest K. Dishner Southwest Texas State University	"Testimony on Teacher Education"
John H. Moore Trinity University	"Quality Issues in Teacher Education"
Eugene W. Kelly, Jr. George Washington University	"Teacher Education in a Learning Society"
Charles N. Beard, Jr. Texas State Teachers Association	"Testimony"
Gene E. Hall Research and Development Center for Teacher Education The University of Texas at Austin	
Preston Kronkosky Southwest Educational Development Laboratory	
Susan Barnes Research and Development Center for Teacher Education The University of Texas at Austin	
Hendrik D. Gideonse University of Cincinnati	
Shirley M. Hord Research and Development Center for Teacher Education The University of Texas at Austin	
Thomas Lasley University of Dayton	
Richard P. Tisher Monash University, Australia	

Austin, Texas

Presenter	Title of Testimony
Frank Crawley The University of Texas at Austin	
Freda Holly Austin Independent School District	
Rowena Stone Round Rock Independent School District	

Atlanta, Georgia

Presenter	Title of Testimony
Jerry Robbins Georgia State University	"Questionable Measures of Quality"
Jane Godfrey Berea College	"Five Areas of Concern in Teacher Education"
Joseph A. Vaughn South Carolina Education Association	
Nancy Cunningham Atlanta Parents and Public Linked for Education	
Ed Deaton Georgia Association of Educators	"Education Excellence"
Robert L. Saunders Memphis State University	"Five-Year Teacher Education Program"
Harold Finkelstein Discovery Learning, Inc.	"Effective Inservice Training"
Edward M. Wolpert Georgia College	"The State's Responsibilities for Teacher Education: Some Views"
Lester Solomon Georgia Department of Education	"Teacher Assessment"
Willis D. Hawley Vanderbilt University	"Undergraduate Teacher Education"

New York City

Presenter	Title of Testimony
Irene Impellizzeri Brooklyn College The City University of New York	"Brooklyn College Teacher Preparation Programs"
Charlotte Frank New York City Board of Education	"Recommendations"
Mary E. Dilworth NAACP Task Force on Teacher Training and Assessment	
Doran Christensen National Council for Accreditation of Teacher Education	
William Dandridge New York University	
Robin Boucher New York University	"A Response to the Excellence Reports"
Leonard S. Blackman Columbia University	"Remarks"
Hugh G. Petrie State University of New York at Buffalo	"Testimony"
Gregory R. Anrig Educational Testing Service	"Views/Recommendations"
Francis X. Sutman Fairleigh Dickinson University	"A Case for Quality Control"
Joe Hasenstab Performance Learning Systems, Inc.	"Teaching as a Performing Art"
Frank B. W. Hawkinshire New York University	"Presentation"
Carol Weinstein Rutgers University	"Testimony"
Maxine Greene Columbia University	"Comments"

New York City

Presenter	Title of Testimony
Lenore H. Ringler New York University	"Statement"
Cecily Cannan Selby New York University	"Teacher Education in Technology"
Jeanne Silver Frankl Public Education Association	"Testimony"
Robert R. Spillane Boston Public Schools	"Testimony"
Anne E. Pooler University of Maine at Orono	"Redesigned Undergraduate Teacher Preparation Program at the University of Maine, Orono: The Clinical Segment"
Paul B. Warren Boston University	"The Quest for Excellence in Education: The Responsibilities of Institutions of Higher Education"
Lia Gelb Bank Street College of Education	"Testimony"
Katherine Sid Seward Park High School	"Testimony"
Hugh J. Scott Hunter College The City University of New York	"Quality and Quality Control in the Teaching Profession"
Hugh G. Petrie State University of New York at Buffalo	"Educational Reform and Teacher Education"
Gladys M. Hannon Community Superintendent Community School District 2, NY	"Comments"
Robert A. Burnham New York University	"Testimony"
Lynn Griesemer Northeast Regional Exchange, Inc.	"Testimony"

New York City

Presenter	Title of Testimony
Robert F. Eagan Connecticut Education Association	"Improving Teacher Education"

Donna Chapin
Board of Education, Shepaug Valley,
    School District #12
Sherman, Connecticut elementary
    school teacher
	"Improving Teacher Education"

San Francisco

Presenter	Title of Testimony
Sue Strand Nevada State Education Association	
Jordan Riak Parents and Teachers Against Violence in Education	

Mark Phillips
San Francisco State University
	"Second-Order Change and the
	    Reconceptualization of the Teacher-
	    Learning Process"

Edna Mitchell Mills College	"Teacher Education at a Crossroad"
Gerald A. Fisher San Francisco State University	"Teacher Education"
Dan Andersen Bonnie Morgan Brigham Young University	"A University-Schools Partnership: Prospects and Promises"
George C. Shaw California Teachers Association	
Trish Stoddart David J. Losk Charles S. Benson University of California, Berkeley	"Some Reflections on the Honorable Profession of Teaching"

San Francisco

Presenter	Title of Testimony
M. Susana Navarro Mexican American Legal Defense and Educational Fund	
Henrietta Schwartz San Francisco State University	"My Vision of the Teaching Profession"
William Gerritz Julia Koppich James W. Guthrie University of California, Berkeley	"Preparing California School Leaders An Analysis of Supply, Demand, and Training"
Fannie Wiley Preston San Francisco State University	"Reform in Teacher Education: The Missing Link"
William Spady Far West Regional Educational Laboratory	

APPENDIX F: Staff

Robert L. Egbert
Project Director
George W. Holmes Professor of Education
University of Nebraska-Lincoln

Stacey Overman
Project Assistant
American Association of Colleges for Teacher Education

James Borgestad
Special Assistant to the President
Office of the General Counsel
University of Minnesota

Mary Kluender
Assistant Professor
University of Nebraska-Lincoln

Sharon Givens
Editor
American Association of Colleges for Teacher Education

Ruth Magann
Designer

Dr. Egbert and Ms. Overman were employed approximately half time by the project. Drs. Kluender and Borgestad assisted during the planning and writing phases. In addition, Martin Haberman, Dean of Urban Outreach at the University of Wisconsin-Milwaukee and former editor of the *Journal of Teacher Education*, freely offered his advice and counsel during the writing phase. Ms. Givens edited the final draft for style and clarity and worked with Ms. Magann to design the report's format.

APPENDIX G: Acknowledgments

No task of this magnitude can be completed without the assistance and contributions of many persons and institutions. At the risk of failing to mention some who should be recognized, we would like to acknowledge the following:

Funding

Initial project funding was from a grant from the United States Department of Education, the Secretary's Discretionary Fund. Additional support was given for specific tasks by the National Institute of Education, the Ford Foundation, the Hewlett Foundation, the Lilly Endowment, and the College of Education at the University of Texas at Austin.

Commissioners

The Commissioners contributed their time for preparation and participation. In some instances they did not even accept reimbursement for expenses.

Hearing Hosts and Paper Presenters

Of thirty-six persons who were asked to host a hearing or prepare and present papers only one was unable to assist the Commission.

Those Who Gave Testimony

Nearly eighty persons voluntarily prepared and presented testimony at the hearings. These persons prepared their testimony, made copies for the Commission and paid all of their own expenses.

Three Universities and the Association

The University of Nebraska-Lincoln, the University of Minnesota, the University of Missouri, and the American Association of Colleges for Teacher Education all contributed substantial amounts of unreimbursed staff time and direct expenses.

APPENDIX H: Reports on Education

College Board. (1983). *Academic Preparation for College*. Princeton, NJ: Author.

Adler, M. J. (1982). *The Paideia Proposal*. New York: Macmillan.

Boyer, E. (1983). *High School*. New York: Harper and Row.

Feistritzer, C. E. (1983). *The Condition of Teaching, A State by State Analysis*. Princeton, NJ: Carnegie Foundation for the Advancement of Teaching.

Forum of Education Organization Leaders. (1983). *Educational Reform: A Response from Education Leaders*. Washington, DC: IEL.

Goodlad, J. (1983). *A Place Called School*. New York: McGraw-Hill.

Merit Pay Task Force Report. (1983). Prepared for the Committee on Education and Labor, House of Representatives. Washington, DC: U.S. Government Printing Office.

National Commission on Excellence in Education. (1983). *A Nation at Risk: The Imperative for Educational Reform*. Washington, DC: U.S. Department of Education.

National Science Board Commission on Precollege Education in Mathematics, Science and Technology. (1983). *Educating Americans for the 21st Century: A Report to the American People and the National Science Board*. Washington, DC: National Science Foundation.

Sanders, T., et al. (1983). *Staffing the Nation's Schools: A National Emergency*. Washington, DC: Council of Chief State School Officers.

Sizer, T. R. (1984). *Horace's Compromise: The Dilemma of the American High School*. Boston: Houghton Mifflin.

Smith, D.C. (1984). *Essential Knowledge for Beginning Teachers*. Washington, DC: Clearinghouse on Teacher Education.

Task Force on Education for Economic Growth. (1983). *Action for Excellence*. Denver: Education Commission of the States.

Task Force on Federal Elementary and Secondary Policy. (1983). *Making the Grade: Report of the Twentieth Century Fund Task Force*. New York: Twentieth Century Fund.